# Knowing God
# Better
# Than Ever

Hofman
474-0776

# Knowing God Better Than Ever

## melody carlson

**by design book 1**

*TH1NK Books*
*an imprint of NavPress®*

TH1NK
P.O. Box 35001
Colorado Springs, Colorado 80935

ISBN 1-57683-725-4

Published in association with the literary agency of Sara A. Fortenberry.

Cover design: Disciple Design
Cover illustration: Collins Dillard, Disciple Design
Creative Team: Gabriel Filkey (s.c.m.), Karen Lee-Thorp, Nicci Jordan, Darla Hightower, Arvid Wallen, Glynese Northam

Printed in Canada

2 3 4 5 6 7 8 9 10 / 09 08 07 06

# contents

# introduction

*D*o you ever feel like your life is spinning out of control? Like no matter what you do, it's all going sideways and you might as well give up? We probably all feel like that sometimes. It's not a good feeling. But what if you could get control of your life? What if you could do something to get your life on track and moving in a direction that you really want to go?

Well, that's just not going to happen on its own. If you want a good life — a life that's fulfilling, exciting, and going somewhere — you need to get on your feet and get involved. And the purpose of this Bible study series is to help you do that.

*You can become the designer of your life.* It's true! You have the power to take a ho-hum existence and transform it into something really amazing. *A designer original!*

Of course, you can't do this without the help of the great Designer — the one who created the heavens and the earth as well as you. But if you're ready for something beyond "hey, whatever," come on along — it's time to start living *By Design!*

# about this series

The *By Design* series was created to help you experience God's Word in a fun, fresh, and personal way. *Knowing God Better Than Ever* is a great book to start with since it's pretty basic and foundational. The topics of the other three books (*Finding Out Who You Really Are, Making the Most of Your Relationships,* and *Discovering a Forgiveness Plan*) were selected for how they specifically relate to what's going on in your life and can be used in any order that appeals to you.

# how to use this book

There are several ways to use this book. You can do it with a group or on your own, whichever works best for you. But sometimes it's easier to stick with something when you do it with friends. And it can be more fun too. If that's the case, you should pick a specific day and time when you'll meet (once a week) to go over that week's chapter together. You should also decide who will take the role of group leader (this helps to keep things rolling in the right direction).

And, naturally, everyone should read and do the writing assignments before getting together. Then when you meet, you can go over the chapter, share your answers or questions, things you've learned, goals you've made, goals you've attained or goals you've blown (no one's perfect). And always make sure you pray for each other during the week. After six weeks, you will not only have completed this Bible study book, but you'll feel a lot closer to your friends too.

As you go through each week's chapter, you can decide what pace works best for you. Some will want to read just a few pages each day, taking time to soak it in and carefully complete the assignments. Others may prefer to do one whole chapter at a sitting—but if that's the case, make sure you go back over it during the rest of the week (consider the Bible verses or goals you've made).

Mostly, you need to discover which way works best for you and then stick with it. And hopefully, as you work through this series, you'll appreciate how God's Word really does have meaning and practical guidance for your life.

# design 101

You're blessed when you stay on course,
walking steadily on the road revealed by GOD.
You're blessed when you follow his directions,
doing your best to find him.

Psalm 119:1-2

*S*uppose you see a very cool dress in a magazine and you can just imagine how it would look on you, and, of course, it's very expensive since it's a designer original — a name you can barely pronounce and don't even want to. And you wonder, *why does this stupid dress have to cost so much?* Maybe the style doesn't even look all that complicated — well, except that it's absolutely perfect.

What you can't see is the time, energy, and imagination that's gone into the production of that simple-looking dress. First of all, a designer had to sit down with a pad and pencil and just think. She considered things like style and line and flow. Then she began sketching some initial ideas. Later she made decisions about the fabric and colors, and then she worked with seamstresses until she got it just right.

But wait a minute; that's not really the beginning. You see, that same designer started out years ago by discovering she had creative talent, and then she went to school, and worked hard — you get the picture. That dress didn't *just* happen.

And neither does your life. Oh, it probably seems like it just happens. Like you get up in the morning, put one foot in front of the other, and finally you're at school sitting comatose in some geometry class, and wishing it was lunchtime. But that is not a designer life. That is a "whatever" life. And if that's good enough for you, then you must've picked up the wrong book.

Because the purpose of this book is to start figuring out what it takes to have a life that's beyond boring, beyond "whatever." So if you want to get some control over your life, and if you want a life that's actually heading somewhere, keep reading. And as you read, ask God to open your ears so you can hear what he's saying about your life. Then, get involved. Roll up your sleeves and do whatever it takes to get this thing going.

> Trust GOD from the bottom of your heart;
> don't try to figure out everything on your own.
> Listen for GOD's voice in everything you do, everywhere you go;
> he's the one who will keep you on track.
> Proverbs 3:5-6

## Design in Progress

One thing you can be sure about is that you'll never *fully arrive*. I mean, living for God is about growing and changing and hopefully becoming more like Jesus. But it doesn't happen overnight or even in a year — it takes a lifetime. The important thing to remember is that every time you fall down, you need to get back up. *God is always there with his hand outstretched, reaching to help you back to your feet. But you need to do your part too.*

## jenna mcallister's story

*My life is out of control, and I know it. It started out simply enough: I told a lie. Not even a big lie.*

"*Sure I can borrow my mom's car to take us to the concert," I promised Krista a couple of days ago. And I thought it would be okay. After all, it was a Christian concert, and my mom had been encouraging me to get more involved in their church's youth group. So really, what was the problem?*

*The problem was that my mom said no. She said it was too far for me to drive at night, and then had the nerve to suggest that my dad might take us. Yeah, sure. I didn't bother to tell Mom that it would be totally lame to "have Daddy drive us." I just acted like everything was cool, no big deal, and then I hoped that Krista would understand when things changed.*

*But by the next day, Krista had invited a couple of girls to join us. Girls that I had been wanting to get to know better. Girls who weren't Christians, but who might be interested in hearing more about God — and why not hear about him through a concert? But not a concert where my dad had to drive us. After all, I was seventeen and had been driving for more than a year. Why couldn't my parents just trust me with this?*

*Feeling torn, I decided to give it one more shot with Mom. Really, she should get this. So, as I dialed Mom's cell phone number, I rehearsed a convincing speech in my head.*

"I'm so glad you called, honey," Mom said quickly. "I have to talk fast because we're about to go through a tunnel. Grandma McAllister had a heart attack this morning. She's okay, but Dad and I are on the way over there, and we won't be home until tomorrow at the soonest. I called Aunt Cindy and she said you can spend the weekend at her house. Sorry to leave you like this, but you can call me on my cell phone and — " She started breaking up before I could say one single word.

I turned off my phone and sighed. I was glad that Grandma McAllister was all right, but this sure messed with my plans. Then I thought for a moment, suddenly wondering if this might not be my big chance. Really, it was like opportunity was knocking on my door. My parents always left spare sets of car keys at home, just in case of emergencies. And, well, this was something of an emergency. How else would Lucy and Anna get a chance to find God? Besides, everyone knows that God works in mysterious ways.

But even as I told Krista the good news, I felt the clenching of guilt in the pit of my stomach. I ignored it.

1. Read the Bible verses in this chapter so far. What advice could Jenna use to do a better job of designing her life?

How can a young person live a clean life?
By carefully reading the map of your Word.
I'm single-minded in pursuit of you;
don't let me miss the road signs you've posted.

Psalm 119:9-10

## The Designer's Direction

You're blessed when you stay on course,
walking steadily on the road revealed by GOD.
You're blessed when you follow his directions,
doing your best to find him.

Psalm 119:1-2

Call it a design plan, a blueprint, or even a road map, but God always has clear direction for you. He wants to show you how to walk with him, how to live your life. You find this direction in his Word (otherwise known as the Bible). But you won't find it if you don't look. And if you don't make a specific plan to look, you surely won't take the time to do it. There's an old saying, if you fail to plan, you plan to fail. *And that's what happens to you when you fail to plan time to get into God's Word.*

## Getting Honest

2. How would you rate your basic understanding of the Bible?

| 0 | 1 | 2 | 3 | 4 | 5 |
|---|---|---|---|---|---|
| No clue. | | | | | I could give college lectures! |

3. How often do you read God's Word? Daily, weekly, never? If you read, how much time do you think you spend reading?

4. List three reasons you should read the Bible more. (The Bible passages in this chapter have suggestions.)

5. What are your one or two best excuses for not reading the Bible as much as you think you should?

6. What can you do to address those obstacles?

## *My Design Plan*

You, GOD, prescribed the right way to live;
now you expect us to live it.
Oh, that my steps might be steady,
keeping to the course you set;
Then I'd never have any regrets
in comparing my life with your counsel.

Psalm 119:4-6

How can you live in the way God has prescribed if you're not listening? How can you know which way the road goes if you're not paying attention to God's direction?

If you're ready to get serious about designing your life, you're ready to get serious about trusting God and getting into his Word. But what if you're totally clueless when it comes to the Bible? What if you don't know Colossians from Revelation? Where do you begin to sort out this humungous old book anyway? And how much are you supposed to read every day? And what if you miss a day? Or a whole week?

First of all, let's keep it simple. It's easier to succeed at something simple than something complicated. And if you're just starting out with the Bible, it's okay to take small bites. In fact, it's okay to take small bites even if you've graduated with a doctorate degree from seminary. The truth is, most people can't absorb too much of God's Word at a time anyway. So why set yourself up to be defeated before you even get started?

The point is to figure out the design plan that works for your life and to make it work for you. And since God is the great designer, make sure you ask him to lead you. *Seven days without God's Word makes one weak.*

## Ask Yourself . . .

7. Am I more of a nighttime or morning person? When am I most alert?

8. Am I more creative or more analytical?

9. Do I learn better in a group or on my own?

10. What do I love to do?

Now try to work who you are into a plan for Bible nutrition. For instance you might be a morning person who is analytical and enjoys groups and being outside. You might consider getting up early and meeting with friends for a time to walk and talk about what you've been reading in the Bible. Or maybe you're a creative night person who learns better while alone and who loves writing poetry. Then why not read the Word at night and write a poem about what you've read? Be open to figuring out ways that make God's Word come alive to you. And don't get locked into a rigid routine. Your life, like seasons, can change. The main thing is to make sure you're taking regular times to be with God and his Word — even if you're doing it in the shower or while walking the dog.

11. A good plan for me might be:

And if you're into God's Word and God's Word is in you, you won't find yourself going in the direction that our friend Jenna seems headed.

## jenna's story continues . . .

*Now throughout the rest of that afternoon, I kept getting this feeling — this little nagging sensation — that what I was planning to do was wrong. But I tried not to listen, or if I listened I just talked myself out of it. Because this wasn't just about me anymore. I now had Krista, Lucy, and Anna to consider, and they were all totally jazzed about going to the city and attending this concert. Already they'd made plans to have dinner at this new Greek restaurant on our way out of town. Lucy had even called ahead to make reservations and offered to treat everyone (which was okay, since we all knew that Lucy's parents were loaded).*

*Of course, Krista and I hadn't mentioned to Lucy and Anna that it was a Christian concert — we didn't want to scare them off. But anyway, I just knew I couldn't let these girls down. They were all looking forward to having a great evening tonight. And, I told myself, my parents would understand if they knew the whole story. My parents were all for sharing the gospel with others. Hadn't they told me that very thing like a million times? So, really, I reassured myself during geometry, what's the big deal?*

*And then I started thinking about what outfit I would wear to the concert (maybe my leather skirt with that new black sweater) and how I'd do my hair — up or down? And what if I looked really cool tonight and actually got the attention of that hottie Andre Hart, lead guitar of Fire'n'Water — the group that was performing? It could happen — our tickets were for seats pretty close to the front. And if not, I could probably meet him when I got his autograph on a CD afterward. Who knew? And so, by the end of geometry, all I could think about was what a totally fun night the four of us would have this evening. Really, what could go wrong?*

I thank you for speaking straight from your heart;
I learn the pattern of your righteous ways.
I'm going to do what you tell me to do;
don't ever walk off and leave me.

Psalm 119:7-8

## *A Cool Rule*

It's better to read *one single Bible verse a day* than to read nothing. Seriously, if you can read and meditate on *one Bible verse a day*, you are doing way better than most people. Sometimes it's helpful to write this verse down on a note card or in a notebook so that you can look back and see ways that God has driven the meaning home for you.

12. Choose one passage from this chapter to copy onto a card and post where you'll see it. If you give it some attention over the course of a week, chances are high that you'll commit it to memory. Then you'll have it where you need it (in your head) when you need it.

### ways to get into the Word

- Join or start a Bible study group.
- Commit to read just one verse a day.
- Write one verse a day on a note card.
- Memorize one verse a week.
- Feel free to underline or make notes in your Bible.
- Start a Bible-verse notebook where you write verses and their meanings.

- Read the gospel of Mark in thirty days.
- Read just Jesus' words in a version of the Bible that puts his words in red.
- If you want a challenge, memorize the order of books in the New Testament.
- If you're really brave, memorize the order of books in the Old Testament.

---

I know what I'm doing. I have it all planned out—
plans to take care of you, not abandon you,
plans to give you the future you hope for.

Jeremiah 29:11

God can do anything, you know—far more than you could ever imagine or
guess or request in your wildest dreams!
He does it not by pushing us around but by working within us,
his Spirit deeply and gently within us.

Ephesians 3:20

# Journal Your Thoughts

Choose either Jeremiah 29:11 or Ephesians 3:20. Write below what those words mean to you. How do those words make you feel? What would you say to God about those words? What questions do you have?

## *My Design Goals*

Okay, so this is your life and you get to work on designing it. What next? Where do you go from here? And how do you get there?

How about setting some goals? They don't need to be huge goals. In fact, it's better to start small — and keep in mind that the Great Designer really has the best plans for you. *Invite him to lead you as you set some goals — or even just one goal.*

You might want to make a goal of having a regular quiet time with God each day. Or you may want to commit to reading from God's Word daily, or creating a prayer list, or joining a fellowship group, or memorizing a verse, or something as simple as making your bed every morning. This is your life and these are your goals.

## *My Goals Are:*

# *Design 101 Final Exam*

Great, you've made it to the end of chapter 1! And maybe you're feeling a little overwhelmed and aren't sure you can even remember everything you've read. But don't worry, this isn't a real test. It's just a chance for you to review what you've read and hopefully see some things more clearly — and maybe you even know yourself a little better. So relax. The following questions don't have right or wrong answers. They're only to help you continue designing your life.

13. How do you feel about the goal(s) you've set for yourself? Are they realistic? Attainable? Do they need revision?

14. Do you have someone in your life (close friend, youth pastor, relative) who you can share your goals with? If so, who is that person? If you don't, what can you do about that?

15. If you were going to make a promise to God, what would it be?

16. Use the space below to write a thank-you prayer.

GOD, teach me lessons for living
so I can stay the course.
Give me insight so I can do what you tell me—
my whole life one long, obedient response.
Psalm 119:33-34

## more bible verses on the basics:

Proverbs 16:1-3
Psalm 37:7
Proverbs 6:20-23
John 16:13-14

# design love

The person who knows my commandments and keeps them, that's who loves me. And the person who loves me will be loved by my Father, and I will love him and make myself plain to him.

John 14:21

You've spent the past week discovering how it's possible to design your life, and you're excited about what might be in store. You also realize that God, the Great Designer, has great plans for you. But maybe you're wondering — *why?* Why does the God of the Universe care about how you live? What difference does it make to him? Why has he gone to all this trouble, giving you directions in his Word? Why should he care about which way your life is headed anyway? Doesn't he have bigger and better things to do?

## Love Is the Key

It all comes down to *love*. God loves you with a forever kind of love — he loved you before you were born, and he will love you for all of eternity. His interest in your life is motivated by pure love. And in return he wants you to love him in the same way.

Love is a great motivator too. Think about it. Is it easier to listen to someone's advice when you (a) can't stand that person, (b) barely respect him, or (c) love and trust him implicitly? That's how God wants you to be with him. He wants you to love and trust him so completely that you want to live your life for him. Because that's how he feels about you — he loves you so completely that he's given everything for you.

> This is how much God loved the world: He gave his Son, his one and only Son. And this is why: so that no one need be destroyed; by believing in him, anyone can have a whole and lasting life.
>
> John 3:16

1. What reasons do you have for believing that God totally loves you?

2. Is there anything that makes you doubt God's love for you? If so, what?

Know this: GOD, your God, is God indeed, a God you can
depend upon. He keeps his covenant of loyal love with those
who love him and observe his commandments
for a thousand generations.

Deuteronomy 7:9

One way you can show your love to God is by spending time with him — by listening to him. But sometimes it's hard to hear him speaking to your heart; sometimes all the noise around you may drown him out. And his voice is a quiet one — he won't yell at you. So you need to learn to *recognize* his voice. But the only way you can learn is by practice — by reading his Word and by taking quiet times to just be with him.

Say you hear this new song on the radio and you totally love it and wish you could sing it. Okay, so maybe your voice isn't that great, but you could at least sing it to yourself in the shower. So how do you learn that song? Well, maybe you buy the CD or you download it into your MP3 player. But the next thing you're doing is playing it — and listening to it. Some lyrics are so tricky that you have to listen to the song over and over until you really get it. But if you want to know the song, you stick with it. Right? And before long, you know the lyrics and the music and you can really cut loose on it — or at least not make a total fool of yourself on karaoke night.

It's not that much different with God. Because you love him, you start downloading his Word (like just one verse) by reading it through a couple of times. Then you study the words more carefully and meditate on them to see what they mean to you personally. Maybe you even write them down so you can remember them better. And then you spend time with God, thinking about this verse and asking him to bring his words to life — to make them part of your life and your beliefs. *And before you know it, the verse is written on your heart — and you totally get it.*

## Words to Live By

Jesus said, "Love the Lord your God with all your passion
and prayer and intelligence." This is the most important,
the first on any list. But there is a second to set alongside it:
"Love others as well as you love yourself." These two commands are pegs;
everything in God's Law and the Prophets hangs from them.

Matthew 22:37-40


This is my command: Love one another the way I loved you.
This is the very best way to love. Put your life on the line for your friends.
You are my friends when you do the things I command you.

John 15:12-14


3. Look at Matthew 22:37-40 and John 15:12-14. What kinds of actions come from real love?

4. Why can't you love God without loving people?

5. Choose one of the Bible passages in this chapter that you really want to download into your brain. Copy it onto a card, and put it somewhere you'll see over and over until you memorize it.

## jenna's story continues . . .

*School was out for the day, and I was riding home with Krista. My phone was turned off just in case my mom decided to call and check on me, but I didn't mention this to Krista.*

*"What's wrong?" asked Krista as she turned down my street. "Why are you being so quiet?"*

*"Huh?" I glanced at her. Krista and I had been best friends since eighth grade, and I usually told her everything. But not this time. "Nothing," I said as I looked out the window and suppressed another surge of guilt.*

*"It's getting cold out," said Krista. "I hope your parents don't get all worried and change their minds about you using the car."*

*"It'll be okay," I said as Krista pulled up at my house.*

*"You'll pick me up around five then?" asked Krista with a bright smile.*

*"Yeah," I called, climbing out of the car. "Later."*

*My feet felt like they had weights tied to them as I walked up to my empty house. Then I saw a light on in the kitchen and suddenly wondered if maybe my parents had come back early after all. But when I got inside, no one was there.*

"It's okay," I told myself as I headed for the phone to call Aunt Cindy. I was doing this for a good reason. Lucy and Anna might even get saved. Who knew? Then I dialed my aunt's number, all ready to give the little speech I'd prepared in my head.

I couldn't believe how easy it was to tell Aunt Cindy that I was spending the night at Krista's.

"I thought you might want to do that," said my aunt. "Are you girls still going to the concert?"

I gulped. "Yeah, that's the plan."

"Good for you," said my aunt.

"Are you guys going too?" I asked, suddenly worried that my aunt and uncle might spoil everything if they found out I was driving.

"No, Emma and Daniel both have colds. It's probably a good thing you're not coming over tonight."

I sighed. "Yeah, probably so."

"How's your grandma?"

"Sounds like she's going to be fine," I said, and then I told her that I had to go. My heart was still pounding hard as I hung up the phone. But I was amazed at how easy that had been. And, like my aunt had said, it was probably a good thing I wasn't spending the night there. In fact, it gave me a whole new idea. So I dialed my mom's cell phone, and when I got the messaging service, I left this message:

"Hi, Mom!" I said brightly. "I just talked to Aunt Cindy and she said Emma and Daniel have the flu so I should probably spend the night at Krista's. I'll see if she can pick me up, but if not, I figured you wouldn't mind if I used the car to drive over. Hope everything's going okay. Tell Grandma hi for me." And when I hung up, I didn't feel all that bad. Okay, I didn't feel all that good, but it wasn't like it was a total lie. And just to *make things better, I decided to call up Krista and see if it was okay to spend the night. Naturally, Krista was cool with that. So it was all set.*

6. How well is Jenna doing at loving God? What makes you say that?

7. How is she doing at loving others? What is she doing that is or isn't loving?

## The Designer's Direction

Keep company with GOD,
get in on the best.
Open up before GOD, keep nothing back;
he'll do whatever needs to be done:
He'll validate your life in the clear light of day
and stamp you with approval at high noon.

Psalm 37:4-6

Do you think God wants to take over your life? Do you think he wants to control you, like he pushes the button and you instantly obey? Of course not! If that had been the case, God would've created robots instead of human beings. But God designed you with a will of your own. He made you able to think for yourself and make your own choices.

His greatest pleasure is when you freely choose to love him. When out of your own free will you come directly to him with arms and heart open wide, and you tell him that you love him! And because you love him, you want to obey him.

Oh sure, you still make mistakes. No one makes perfect choices all the time. But the more you get to know God, the more you will love him, and consequently, the less you will blow it. Or when you do blow it, you'll be sorrier sooner and you'll come running back to God to make things right.

## Getting Honest

8. How would you rate your level of love for God?

| 0 | 1 | 2 | 3 | 4 | 5 |
|---|---|---|---|---|---|

Icy cold.                                                    On fire!

9. Are you content with this level? Why or why not?

10. Does your love level affect how much time you spend alone with God? If so, how?

11. What is typically the first thing you say to God when you come before him?

12. List three things you can do that will express your love to God in a fresh new way.

## My Design Plan

Good friend, take to heart what I'm telling you;
collect my counsels and guard them with your life.
Tune your ears to the world of Wisdom;
set your heart on a life of Understanding.
That's right—if you make Insight your priority,
and won't take no for an answer,
Searching for it like a prospector panning for gold,
like an adventurer on a treasure hunt,
Believe me, before you know it Fear-of-God will be yours;
you'll have come upon the Knowledge of God.

Proverbs 2:1-5

Do you get the feeling that God has good things just waiting for you? More love than you've ever known before? More acceptance and forgiveness than you can even imagine? Because he loves you, God has amazing things in store for you.

But *God will not force these good things down your throat.* He wants you to come to him, seek him out, wait on him, listen to him, and obey him. It's like even though he's the Great Designer, it's up to you to partner with him. He won't force his designs on anyone. No, that would be too boring — too mechanical. He prefers for you to live your life fully, making choices, learning lessons, and coming to him again and again for guidance. And all this is motivated by love!

Can you see a design plan for your life beginning to emerge yet? Maybe you sense that he's calling you to a higher level of life than what you've been experiencing. Maybe you're starting to see, for a refreshing change, that you actually have some control in your life—and that's feeling pretty cool. Perhaps you've noticed that your love for God has helped you make better choices lately. Have you noticed anything changing about you?

Or maybe you've blown it. Maybe you've forgotten your goals and are feeling more like a loser than ever. Well, don't give up! Sometimes things have to get messy before you get really serious and start cleaning them up. Just don't let them get too messy. Because, like it or not, sometimes one bad choice simply leads to another.

But instead of focusing on your failure, remind yourself that you love God. And know that nothing pleases God more than when you come before him with an honest heart that's filled with love.

> So be very careful to act exactly as GOD commands you.
> Don't veer off to the right or the left.
> Walk straight down the road GOD commands so that
> you'll have a good life and live a long time
> in the land that you're about to possess.
> Deuteronomy 5:32-33

*Ask Yourself . . .*

13. Did I spend any quiet time with God today? If not, why not?

14. What motivates me in my relationship with God?

15. Do I honestly believe that I need God's direction in my life? Or do I still think I can do better on my own?

*Journal Your Thoughts*

"Give your entire attention to what God is doing right now,
and don't get worked up about what may or may not happen tomorrow.
God will help you deal with whatever
hard things come up when the time comes."

Matthew 6:34

When you love someone you usually don't have a problem giving that person "your entire attention." Consider Matthew 6:34. What would motivate you to give "your entire attention to what God is doing right now"? Write a few sentences about how Jesus' words make you feel.

## *My Design Goals*

Look back at the goals you listed in chapter 1. Do you want to keep going with them, or do you want to revise them in any way?

For instance, you might revise them to focus on what you need to do today. (Do you need to forgive yourself for yesterday and move on?) You might review them to make sure they're motivated by love for God and others.

Consider these things as you revise your goals or write new ones.

### *My Revised Goals Are:*

## *This Week's Final Exam*

Congratulations, you've made it through chapter 2. Some people say it only takes two weeks to make a habit. Do you think you've had enough time to create the habit of loving God and listening to him? Well, hopefully, you're off to a good start. But, if you're like most people, it will take the rest of your life to keep this thing going. That's just how it works. So take some time to finish the following exercise, and then pat yourself on the back for having made it this far. Because, whether you can see it or not, your life must be changing in all sorts of ways!

16. Can you see anything about yourself or your life that seems to be changing or improving? If so, what?

17. Have you told anyone how you're doing on designing your life? If so, how has that gone for you?

18. Remember the promise you made to God at the end of chapter 1? Have you been able to keep it? Do you need to make it again? Or do you need to make a new one?

19. Once again, use the space below to write a thank-you prayer.

## additional bible verses on love:

Psalm 18:1-3

Psalm 42:1-2

# design  devotion

GOD, O God of Israel, there is no God like you in the skies above
or on the earth below, who unswervingly keeps covenant with his
servants and unfailingly loves them while they sincerely
live in obedience to your way.

2 Chronicles 6:14

*O*kay, you've covered the basic foundation of designing your life. That foundation is kind of like the dress designer discovering that she has natural talent and then getting her training. But to really get down to the work of designing a dress, she needs some basic supplies. She needs things like fabric, notions, scissors, and a sewing machine to turn a design idea into a real dress.

So now it's time for you to acquire some basic supplies too. The next four chapters on devotion, prayer, fellowship, and discipline should provide you with what you need to continue making your designer life.

Maybe you're wondering, what is devotion? According to Webster's, *devotion* is an earnest attachment to a cause or person, profound dedication, consecration, observance or worship, a form of prayer. In other words, it means a lot. But think about it: When you're devoted to something or someone, how do you act? Do you think about that person a lot, do you do special things for that person, do you care a lot about what that person thinks of you? If you're really devoted, you do.

That's what God wants from you. He wants you to be completely devoted to him. And that's a big commitment. But here's what makes it work—God has designed you to be that way. He has made you with a need to worship him, to spend time with him, and to enjoy an ongoing friendship with him. In fact, when you deny yourself these things, you end up frustrated, confused, and depressed. It's God's way of reminding you that you need him. And you need to be devoted to him.

But how do you do this? How can you live out a life of real devotion in the midst of a culture that tends to forget about God? Do you have to turn yourself into a freak or wear strange clothes or start up some weird kind of group to show that you're really, truly devoted?

Of course not. You just need to focus your heart on God, spend regular times reading his Word, and continue to grow in your love for him. God's love for you is beyond anything you can imagine, and he longs for you to love him with the same kind of passion and attention you might give to a major crush—and even more! God wants you to fall head over heels for him, so much so that you can't wait to spend time with him—whether it's a brief "I love you, Lord!" while you're getting on the bus, or pouring out your heart for thirty minutes on your knees.

And when you surrender your heart to God like this, you'll discover lots of cool rewards. God's peace is a huge reward. So is his guidance and wisdom. And knowing that he loves you, and stays by your side even when situations get messy, is a huge comfort. Being devoted to God is as much about blessing your life as it is about blessing him.

"When you call on me, when you come and pray to me, I'll listen.

When you come looking for me, you'll find me.

Yes, when you get serious about finding me

and want it more than anything else . . . "

Jeremiah 29:12-13

What keeps you from finding God? Or is he even lost? Everyone has distractions that pull them away from spending time with God. What are yours? Do you get caught up in the latest reality show or spend hours on the computer? Are you always checking your e-mail, looking for that latest instant message? Is it a boyfriend that consumes you, a fashion fetish, or just plain laziness? Do you mindlessly play video games or pore through magazines? Seriously, there are plenty of distractions out there. You don't even have to go looking. It's like our culture just throws them at us, one after the other.

And it's not that any of these things are necessarily bad for you. But they may not be the best for you. And they are wrong if they keep you from spending time with God. Distractions are like counterfeits. They set themselves up as something good and desirable but at the same time steal what you really need. Like God.

Think about it — the Creator of the Universe totally loves you! He's given everything to have a relationship with you. And that's way more exciting than the latest video game, way more fulfilling than the hottest movie — and believe it or not even the coolest boyfriend cannot begin to compete with what God has to offer you. So, really, why would you settle for a counterfeit when God is standing at the door and just waiting for you to let him in?

1. What distractions pull your attention away from God? Check the ones that apply and list a few of your own.

- ☐ TV
- ☐ Video games
- ☐ My appearance
- ☐ Boy(s)
- ☐ Trying to be popular
- ☐ Fashion
- ☐ Music
- ☐ _____
- ☐ _____
- ☐ _____

Now that you can see what your distractions are, can you admit that they aren't equal to God? That nothing and no one will ever be equal to God? Or do you honestly feel that the things you've listed above really should take priority over the Lord of the Universe, Lover of your soul, Almighty God? Are you really willing to close the door in his face just so you can catch the latest reality show on the boob tube?

Think about this: What if you put as much energy and enthusiasm into following God as you do in some of the boxes you just checked? Can you imagine how that kind of devotion could change your life?

2. Take a few minutes, right now, to give your list to God. Ask him to show you what you should do about these distractions. Then trust him to lead you. Write out your prayer below.

## spiritual checkup

If someone were to give you a spiritual checkup today, how would you be doing? Is your relationship with God healthy and vigorous? Or is it feeling a little weak and washed out? Or perhaps it's in serious peril, maybe in need of a transfusion. Can you see how your spiritual condition may be the direct result of both the quantity and quality of time that you spend with God?

To see how fit you really are, rank the following activities according to these numbers: (1) dead, (2) barely breathing, (3) existing, (4) fairly okay, (5) alive and feeling good.

_____ Reading God's Word

_____ Spending time alone with God

_____ Praying

_____ Obeying God

_____ Memorizing verses

_____ Having fellowship with other Christians

_____ Worshiping God

_____ Meditating on God's Word

_____ Thanking God

_____ Meeting my goals from the past two weeks

So add up your score now, and let's see how you're doing.

**0–10 points** — You're in trouble. It's time to call the spiritual undertaker or ask God to bring you back to life, because you are like spiritually dead.

**11–20 points** — Hold on, maybe you can get someone to do some spiritual CPR, or ask God to give you a transfusion, because you are almost a goner.

**21–30 points** — Well, life's probably not too fun or fulfilling, but at least you haven't given up completely. Even so, if things don't change, you'll be toast before long.

**31–40 points** — Okay, it looks like you're trying. And don't feel bad, you should at least have enough energy to make some great improvements this week.

**41–50 points** — All right, you are going for it. Not only are you giving it your most, but you are probably getting the most out of it too. Live, breathe, be healthy!

---

## jenna's story continues . . .

*Later that afternoon, I dressed carefully for the concert. I put on my leather skirt and a cool pair of boots as well as the new black sweater that looks so great with my hair. And when I checked myself out in the mirror, I could tell I looked good. Really good. Unfortunately, I didn't feel that good. In fact, I was getting a bit of a stomachache. But I wasn't going to think about that right now. I still needed to feed the cat and lock up the house and all the normal responsible things my parents expected me to do.*

*"It's girls' night out," I told myself as I grabbed my bag and the spare set of car keys. "Time to have some fun."*

*And why shouldn't I have some fun? I asked myself as I went out to the garage. After all, I was a hard worker. I got good grades, helped out at home, and even volunteered in the church nursery every other Sunday. Didn't I deserve a little fun? And we were going to a Christian concert, and I was taking two girls who weren't even Christians. How much better could it get?*

When I got into the car, I noticed Mom's leather Bible in the passenger's seat. As I picked it up to slide beneath her seat, a church bulletin fell into my lap. Despite myself, I couldn't help reading the weekly Bible verse printed across the front of the flyer in bold black ink:

"The person who knows my commandments and keeps them, that's who loves me. And the person who loves me will be loved by my Father, and I will love him and make myself plain to him." John 14:21

I felt a tightening across my chest, but instead of pausing to consider its source or even the words on the bulletin, I simply stuffed both Bible and bulletin beneath my seat. Then I pushed the garage door opener button and started the car. My hands were shaking just slightly. But I took a deep breath and told myself to just chill. Then I carefully backed out.

Before long I was driving down the street with the CD player pumping out one of my favorite songs, and I felt certain that everything was going to be perfectly fine. Okay, mostly certain. There was still a small part of me that felt somewhat guilty. But I was doing my best to keep that little voice quiet.

God is love. When we take up permanent residence in a life of love, we live in God and God lives in us. This way, love has the run of the house, becomes at home and mature in us, so that we're free of worry on Judgment Day—our standing in the world is identical with Christ's. There is no room in love for fear. Well-formed love banishes fear. Since fear is crippling, a fearful life—fear of death, fear of judgment— is one not yet fully formed in love.

We, though, are going to love—love and be loved. First we were loved, now we love. He loved us first.

1 John 4:17-19

3. Think about 1 John 4:17-19. God's love is supposed to push the fear out of your life. How does that work for you?

4. Think about Jenna. Should she be afraid? Why or why not?

## The Designer's Direction

That's why we can be so sure that every detail in our lives
of love for God is worked into something good.

God knew what he was doing from the very beginning.
He decided from the outset to shape the lives of those who love him along
the same lines as the life of his Son. The Son stands first
in the line of humanity he restored. We see the original
and intended shape of our lives there in him.

Romans 8:28-29

Do you believe God only wants the *best* for you? Think about that question before you answer it. Seriously, do you believe that God loves you so much that he wants what is the very best for you?

Well, he does! Unfortunately, you don't always know what the best things are for yourself. Like you see something that you think you must have—something that you're certain will make you supremely happy. Maybe it's a great pair of shoes or a designer bag. Or maybe it's going out with a guy you think is awesome. It could even be something as seemingly selfless as wanting a loved one to get well.

But the thing is, you're *not* God. You're *not* in his head, and you do *not* know what he knows. You never will. As a result, *you don't always know what's really best for you and everybody else.* Sure, if you listen to God and stay tuned to his Word, you will know how to make good choices that will ultimately be in your best interest. But only God knows what's truly the very best for you. That's why you need to trust him.

> After God made that decision of what his children should be like,
> he followed it up by calling people by name. After he called
> them by name, he set them on a solid basis with himself.
> And then, after getting them established, he stayed with them
> to the end, gloriously completing what he had begun.
>
> So, what do you think? With God on our side like this, how can we lose?
> If God didn't hesitate to put everything on the line for us, embracing our
> condition and exposing himself to the
> worst by sending his own Son, is there anything else
> he wouldn't gladly and freely do for us?
> Romans 8:30-32

In other words, *God is totally devoted to you.* Not only did he create you (so that you could have an ongoing friendship with him), but he created a way to forgive you when you blew it so badly that your friendship with him could've been ruined forever. If God is so devoted to you that he gave his son's life to remove your sins, wouldn't you want to be as devoted as possible to him?

5. How would you rank your level of devotion to God right now?
   a. I want to love and serve God with every ounce of my being.
   b. I respect God and want to live a good life for him.
   c. I believe in God, and someday I'll become more devoted.
   d. I'm not sure how I feel about God right now.
   e. My devotion is with someone or something else. Not God.

6. Are you satisfied with this level of devotion? If not, what level would you rather be at?

7. What can you do to change your level?

"Because a loveless world," said Jesus, "is a sightless world.
If anyone loves me, he will carefully keep my word and
my Father will love him—we'll move right into the neighborhood!
Not loving me means not keeping my words. The message you are hearing
isn't mine. It's the message of the Father who sent me."

John 14:23-24

If you look at John 14:23-24, you can see that love and obedience go hand in hand. In fact, if you were to redefine devotion (when it comes to God), love + obedience could be your secret formula. Most of the time, it's easy to have good feelings about God. But it's not always easy to obey him. Yet how can you say you love him if you don't obey him? His Word says over and over that these things must go together. So as you set yourself to devotion, you must bind love and obedience together. And as you do this you'll discover why it's so important—because it makes your life so much better. Sure, it might not eliminate all the bumps along the way, but it will go a whole lot more smoothly—and the ride's a lot more fun!

## My Design Plan

Now that you know a designer life doesn't just happen without plans, you can probably understand that you need a plan for devotion too. Maybe your plan is simply to get up a little earlier in the morning so that you can spend time with God. Or maybe it's to turn off the computer in the evening to set aside some quiet time just between you and God. But whatever your plan is, it must involve action on your part.

You're unique, so you need to discover the best way for you to spend time with God. Time with God doesn't have to be the same for everyone. Think about the way God made you, and then try to set up a devotional time that fits who you are. Consider these things:

8. You feel close to God *where* (In your room, beneath a tree, in a closet, bicycling . . . )?

9. You feel most spiritually alert *when* (Morning, noon, night . . . )?

10. You respond to *what* (Reading, music, art, poetry, audio teaching . . . )?

Now try to think of ways to incorporate the elements that work for you into your devotional time. Ask God to help you get ideas. Write your ideas in the section below (Goals Again). Don't give yourself any excuses to fail, but when you blow it, just confess it to God, accept his forgiveness, forgive yourself, and get back on track.

## Goals Again

Take another look at your goals. Is it time to make new ones or recommit to the old ones? Maybe you want to focus on just one goal, like the devotional plan you've been working on. Make it specific. If your goal is to have a quiet time with God, make sure you say *what time* and *how often* you will do this. Then you can measure whether you're reaching your goal or not.

My goal for devotional time is:

Other goals that are still important to me are:

*Journal Your Thoughts*

Read Jeremiah 29:12-13 again on page 45. What is God saying to you through this passage? What do you want to say back to him? Consider memorizing these verses.

## additional bible verses on devotion:

2 John 1:6
1 John 4:15-16
Mark 12:29-30

Good friend, don't forget all I've taught you;

take to heart my commands.

They'll help you live a long, long time

a long life lived full and well.

Proverbs 3:1-2

# design  prayer

"I am the Vine, you are the branches. When you're joined
with me and I with you, the relation intimate and organic,
the harvest is sure to be abundant. Separated, you can't produce a
thing. . . . But if you make yourselves at home with me and
my words are at home in you, you can be sure that
whatever you ask will be listened to and acted upon."

John 15:5,7

*P*raying doesn't come easy for everyone. In fact, the mere thought of praying is overwhelming for lots of people. But it might be that you make praying too complicated. Somehow you get this crazy idea that prayers must be said in this certain way at this certain time with words that sound just right. But real prayer isn't like that.

*Real prayer is simply a direct communication between you and God—straight from the heart.* In other words, it's just a conversation you have with God, the same way you would talk to your best friend. Okay, maybe God doesn't answer like your best friend (in an audible voice), but be assured, *he is listening.* And his answers will come . . . in time.

You live in a culture where communication is a top priority. Seriously, you can hardly get away from it. Whether you're talking on a cell phone or chatting online or actually having face-to-face conversations, you spend a large portion of your day just communicating. And communication is good. Imagine what it would be like not to hear from your best friend for a few days or even a few weeks. You would probably get worried at first. Then you might be hurt and assume she was mad at you or even hated your guts. And if she quit talking to you completely, you probably wouldn't be best friends anymore. A friendship without communication cannot last.

In the same way, how can you expect to maintain a friendship with God if you don't talk to him? And God really does want to be your best friend. He wants to be the one you take your problems to. And he doesn't want you to make up flowery speeches that sound all perfect and nice. No, he just wants you to get real with him — to simply relax and be yourself.

So why make praying complicated? Prayer is talking to God. That's all. And you can tell him anything and everything. Because *there's no way you can shock God.* He's been around a long, long time and has heard it all. But he loves you and is just waiting for you to come and pour out your heart to him.

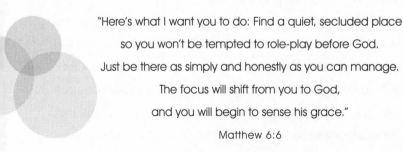

"Here's what I want you to do: Find a quiet, secluded place
so you won't be tempted to role-play before God.
Just be there as simply and honestly as you can manage.
The focus will shift from you to God,
and you will begin to sense his grace."

Matthew 6:6

1. Imagine you're somewhere by yourself (in a room, closet, under a tree) and you're talking to God like he's your best friend. How does that make you feel?

2. Now consider what you would say (if God was your best friend). Would you tell him about what's worrying you? Would you tell him about an old hurt? Would you ask him to help you with something? Write down what you'd like to talk about.

Okay, so maybe you're feeling more sold on the idea of praying now. You're starting to relax and accept that prayer is just talking to God. But maybe you talk for five minutes, and suddenly you feel like you don't have much to say. Don't worry, lots of people feel like that. Maybe that's why Jesus taught his followers how to pray. But he probably didn't want them to mimic the exact words of his prayer as much as he wanted them to see that there are many kinds of things they can talk to God about.

## *Our Example*

"Our Father in heaven
Reveal who you are.
Set the world right;
Do what's best—
as above, so below.
Keep us alive with three square meals.
Keep us forgiven with you and forgiving others.
Keep us safe from ourselves and the Devil.
You're in charge!
You can do anything you want!
You're ablaze in beauty!
Yes. Yes. Yes."

Matthew 6:9-13

The prayer Jesus taught his followers in Matthew 6:10-13 includes basic elements that you can include in your own prayers. You can break down the words of Jesus' prayer to learn how to personalize the same kind of meaning into your own prayers. Here is a list of the general things that Jesus prayed:

1. Acknowledge who God is (our Father in heaven).
2. Ask him to reveal himself to you.
3. Ask him to reveal himself to those around you.
4. Ask him to do what's best for you and others.
5. Ask him to give you what you need to survive (food and so on).
6. Ask him to forgive you and to help you forgive others.
7. Ask him to protect you from things that could hurt you.

8. Acknowledge that God is in charge.
9. Praise him that he can do anything.
10. Praise him for being God.

## Design in Progress

So you realize that prayer is simply talking to God, and you have Jesus' example of prayer. But maybe you still feel a little inhibited. Like where do you go from here? Maybe it would help to design your own prayer.

3. Using the ten elements of Jesus' prayer listed above, write out a ten-sentence prayer of your own.

1.

2.

3.

4.

5.

6.

7.

8.

9.


10.


Amen! (Yes! Yes! Yes!)


## Pray All the Time

Be cheerful no matter what; **pray all the time;**
thank God no matter what happens.
This is the way God wants you who belong to Christ Jesus to live.
1 Thessalonians 5:16-18 (emphasis added)


*Pray all the time?* Maybe you're wondering what's up with that. Or how it's even possible. But that's really what God wants from you. He wants you to be able to turn to him at any moment — whether you're in the middle of a conversation with a friend, or taking a biology test, or standing in line at McDonald's, or playing soccer, or whatever. God wants you to be ready and willing to come to him with your thoughts, concerns, worries, thanks, and praises *all the time.*

Of course, this kind of relationship doesn't happen overnight. But as you get in the habit of praying off and on throughout the day, you'll begin to realize that *the more you pray, the more you pray.* And the more you pray, the more normal it feels. Pretty soon you do it almost without thinking. It's like you're really getting tuned into God. And, man, does that feel good!

But what happens when you can't pray — when you've stepped away from God and put yourself in a place where you're worried he won't be listening? Let's check on Jenna.

## jenna's story continues . . .

*I tried to focus on the fast-moving conversation of my three friends as I drove them across town. Krista, Anna, and Lucy were definitely jazzed about tonight. I wished I could capture the same kind of enthusiasm, but all I could think about was, What if something goes wrong? What if I get in trouble? Why was I doing this? But how could I stop this thing without looking totally lame?*

*"Hey, there's the restaurant," said Lucy loudly. "Right there on the left. See the sign, Jenna?" So I slowed down, put on my signal, then waited for traffic to clear before I turned into Malini's parking lot.*

*"This place looks good," said Krista as we got out of the car.*

*"Man, it's getting really cold out," said Lucy. Just then an icy wind whipped some pieces of debris across the parking lot, and we hurried over to the entrance.*

*"My dad said it might snow tonight," said Anna.*

*"Seriously?" I asked. "Snow?"*

*Anna laughed. "Don't worry. My dad's never right about this kind of thing."*

*Even so, I did feel worried. And as my friends ordered all kinds of interesting and exotic foods, my stomach seemed to be tying itself into tight little knots.*

*"How about you?" asked the waitress when my turn came.*

*"I — uh — " I looked stupidly around me. I hadn't even made a decision yet. "I'll have what she's having," I said quickly, pointing at*

*Krista. Of course, this made my friends laugh, but the waitress seemed satisfied as she jotted something down, although I had no idea what I'd actually ordered.*

*The words of my friends seemed to float right over my head like I wasn't even there, or maybe I was having some sort of out-of-body experience.*

*"Earth to Jenna," said Krista as she elbowed me.*

*"Huh?" I turned and looked at my best friend.*

*"Man, you are really checked out," said Lucy.*

*"Been drinking?" teased Anna.*

*"Yeah, you bet," I said.*

*"It's like you're somewhere else," said Krista.*

*"Sorry." I shrugged. "Guess I was kinda spaced."*

*Then the food came, and I tried to look interested in the strange-looking dish that was placed in front of me. I wanted to ask Krista what she was eating, but I didn't feel the need to look any more stupid than I already felt. Instead I picked at my spicy food since my stomach was too much of a mess to actually eat anyway. But the other girls seemed to enjoy their meals, and they even ordered dessert.*

*Finally it was time to head to the concert. It was already dark when we went outside and even colder than when we'd arrived. It did feel like it could snow tonight. But I said nothing as I climbed back into the driver's seat and turned the key in the ignition.*

*The three girls seemed even more wound up as I headed for the freeway entrance that would take us to the city where the concert was being held. But I said nothing as I focused all my attention on driving. I wondered if this kind of stress and anxiety could make a person physically ill. Because I was starting to feel literally sick to my stomach, like I might* hurl any minute. *Just focus on the road*, I told myself. *Just focus on your driving.*

I really wanted to pray. That's what I would normally do when I felt this stressed. But how could I ask God to help me when I knew that I had already blown it — blown it big time? And intentionally too! Why would God want to help me now?

Despite my chattering friends in the car, I felt more alone than ever. My stomach was knotted and my head was starting to throb, but worst of all I felt like I had totally turned my back on God. And that was making me more miserable than anything. But other than pulling over — and it would be unsafe to pull over on the freeway — what could I do?

And so I told myself that I was just getting paranoid for no good reason. I rationalized, after all, that I was taking my friends to a Christian concert, and that this evening might even be a life-changing experience for Anna and Lucy. I told myself to quit freaking and just chill. Everything was going to be perfectly fine.

And then I saw flashing red lights up ahead. And cars that were not moving at all. The problem was, I was going nearly sixty miles an hour, and when I stomped on the brakes the car began to skid. And then it slid sideways. And the terrified screams of my three friends filled the interior of the car and I knew that it was too late.

"God, help us!" shrieked Krista.

4. Do you think God is listening to Krista? Will he help them? What makes you say that?

5. Have you ever been in a situation where you felt there was no point in praying because God wouldn't listen? If so, when?

Don't fret or worry. Instead of worrying, pray.
Let petitions and praises shape your worries into prayers,
letting God know your concerns. Before you know it,
a sense of God's wholeness, everything coming together for good,
will come and settle you down. It's wonderful what happens
when Christ displaces worry at the center of your life.

Summing it all up, friends, I'd say you'll do best by filling your minds and
meditating on things true, noble, reputable, authentic, compelling,
gracious—the best, not the worst; the beautiful,
not the ugly; things to praise, not things to curse.

Philippians 4:6-8

6. What benefits of prayer do you see in Philippians 4:6-8?

7. Why do you think Paul (the writer of Philippians) makes such a big deal about what you fill your mind with?

8. What are some things you think about a lot that maybe Paul would say you should dump?

Living in a time when the world seems tightly packed with trouble, it's easy to worry. Oh, no one likes to admit that they worry, but sometimes it's hard not to feel anxious or uptight. Especially if you pay attention to the news media, which can blow anything totally out of proportion.

But God gives you prayer as a remedy for your anxiety. He offers you the chance to pray about everything — instead of worrying. Because, think about it, what good does it do to worry? It doesn't change anything. It just makes you feel like crud. Why not pray instead? Because prayer not only changes things — it changes you!

> Are you hurting? Pray. Do you feel great? Sing. Are you sick?
> Call the church leaders together to pray. . . .
> Believing-prayer will heal you, and Jesus will put you on your feet.
> And if you've sinned, you'll be forgiven—healed inside and out.

Make this your common practice: Confess your sins to each other
and pray for each other so that you can live together whole
and healed. The prayer of a person living right with
God is something powerful to be reckoned with.

James 5:13-16

## My Design Plan

As always, it's up to you. You can see there is good reason to pray. Maybe you've even experienced the rewards of praying already. But it's up to you to design and sustain an ongoing prayer life. No one can do it but you. And the only way you can do it is to *just do it*.

Maybe you begin by making sure that you're having your daily quiet time. You make sure that you're spending time in God's Word and talking to him. But don't limit your prayers to just once a day. Think how you'd feel if your best friend was only willing to talk to you once a day — say, every morning from 7:15 to 7:30. That is, if she remembered to call. How would you feel about that? How do you think that makes God feel?

Jesus was matter-of-fact: "Embrace this God-life.
Really embrace it, and nothing will be too much for you.
This mountain, for instance: Just say, 'Go jump in the lake'—
no shuffling or shilly-shallying—and it's as good as done.
That's why I urge you to pray for absolutely everything,
ranging from small to large. Include everything as you
embrace this God-life, and you'll get God's everything.
And when you assume the posture of prayer, remember that

it's not all *asking.* If you have anything against someone, *forgive*—only then will your heavenly Father be inclined to also wipe your slate clean of sins."

Mark 11:22-25

*Ask Yourself...*

9.  What does God want from me?

10. What do I want from God?

11. How could prayer change my life?

From now on, whatever you request along the lines of
who I am and what I am doing, I'll do it.
That's how the Father will be seen for who he is in the Son.
I mean it.
John 14:13

12. John 14:13 says I should pray "along the lines" of who Jesus is and what he's doing. What can I ask for that fits who he is and what he's doing?

## Journal Your Thoughts

Use this space to write whatever is on your mind about prayer right now — reasons why you believe it's important, questions you still have about prayer, nagging fears, or things you're excited about.

## *My Design Goals for Praying*

Okay, you've heard that you need to keep your prayers simple, but that you need to pray all the time. What specific things can you do to help yourself remember to pray? Brainstorm some ideas, anything from writing a reminder on your hand to memorizing a verse about prayer.

### additional bible verses on prayer:

Psalm 66:17-20
Matthew 6:7-9
Mark 11:24
Luke 18:10-14
1 Timothy 2:1-3
Jude 1:20-21

# design  fellowship

*Let's see how inventive we can be in encouraging love and helping out,*

*not avoiding worshiping together as some do but spurring each other on,*

*especially as we see the big Day approaching.*

Hebrews 10:24-25

*C*an you imagine how it would feel to be without even one friend? Maybe you've been there, done that. Maybe you're actually doing it right now. The point is, it's not much fun, is it? And it's not the plan God has for your life. He's designed you to be a social person. He's made you so that you get lonely and blue if you spend too much time in isolation. You instinctively know that something's not right. And that's because he wants you to get out there and enjoy some fellowship.

But what is fellowship? Does it mean joining a club or going to youth group or attending weekly Bible studies? Does it mean joining a church and showing up every time the doors are open? Maybe. Maybe not.

Fellowship is really about spending good times with Christian friends—friends who think like you do, who care about the kinds of things you care about, and who share some common ground with you—friends who basically encourage you to live the best life possible.

Because everyone is unique, the way you have fellowship can be unique too. For one person it could mean starting a Bible study during lunch break. For someone else it might mean hanging with Christian friends at a basketball game. For some it will be joining some kind of Christian youth group or volunteering to help out at the local soup kitchen. However you choose to do it, *fellowship means connecting with Christians.* Fellowship is making good friends — friends who, like you, are learning how to really live their lives for God.

Does this mean you don't associate with kids who aren't Christians? Of course, not! God wants you to be light wherever you are. But hanging with friends who don't believe doesn't meet your need for fellowship. And you can't expect kids who don't share your faith to understand what you're going through as a Christian. When you need a good friend, someone who really understands you and the challenges you're facing, and will stick by you through good times and bad, you can usually depend on a Christian.

That doesn't mean Christian friends never blow it. You're human, right? You blow it — a lot. But hopefully, you can see and admit your mistakes, ask for forgiveness, and get smarter for the next go 'round. And God expects you to forgive your Christian friends in the same way he forgives you — totally.

## Loving Imperfect People

My beloved friends, let us continue to love each other
since love comes from God.
Everyone who loves is born of God
and experiences a relationship with God.
The person who refuses to love

doesn't know the first thing about God,
because God *is* love—so you can't know him
if you don't love.

1 John 4:7-8

So does this mean that it's *easy* to love someone just because he or she is a Christian? No way! Some Christians can be the hardest people on the planet to love. They can make you want to pull your hair out and scream. You need to love them anyway.

But just because you love them doesn't mean you have to love what they do. Like what if you know this Christian girl who acts all superior and judgmental toward nonbelievers, and it makes you sick—do you have to love *that*? Of course not. But you do have to love *her*.

You may need to ask God to help you love this girl. Especially since the loving thing to do might be to talk to her and tell her that you're concerned about the way she treats others. But check yourself and make sure you express something like this in love, or you could end up becoming just like her.

Anyone who hates a brother or sister is a murderer. . . .

This is how we've come to understand and experience love:
Christ sacrificed his life for us. This is why we ought to live
sacrificially for our fellow believers, and not just be out for ourselves.
If you see some brother or sister in need and have the means to
do something about it but turn a cold shoulder and do nothing,
what happens to God's love? It disappears.
And you made it disappear.

1 John 3:15-17

1. From the Bible passages in this chapter so far, how would you describe what it means to love a fellow Christian?

2. What if, instead of hating somebody, you simply don't care about them one way or the other? What's wrong with that?

3. Do you know someone who's hard to love? If so, what do you plan to do about it?

Don't push your way to the front;

don't sweet-talk your way to the top.

Put yourself aside, and help others get ahead.

Don't be obsessed with getting your own advantage.

Forget yourselves long enough to lend a helping hand.

Philippians 2:3-4

4. Do you have a situation where you want to push your way to the top? If so, how can you live the way Philippians 2:3-4 describes?

5. Have you ever felt used by a "friend"? If you have, what kind of friend does that make you want to be?

Sometimes you don't know who your real friends are until you really need them. Jenna is about to see this up close.

## jenna's story continues . . .

*It was like a dream — a very bad dream. On one hand it was as if we were moving in slow motion. As the car spun in a circle on the freeway, I could see snowflakes mixed with red taillights, all swirling around and around. But the taillights got closer with each turn, and in the background, I could hear the screams of my terrified friends and the frantic prayers of Krista. And in those split seconds, I knew it was unavoidable.*

*We would eventually hit something.*

*Then it happened. A loud crash, followed by a jolting stop that slammed me against the door. The car was stopped dead, the driver's side planted against what appeared to be a semitrailer just moments before we hit. Shattered glass was everywhere and I was still clutching the steering* wheel as I tried to see what exactly had happened, but with deflated airbags and some kind of white powder all over the place, everything appeared kind of murky and unreal.

"Are you guys okay?" I yelled.

"I think I'm alright," Lucy said from the backseat.

"Me too," said Anna in a tiny voice.

"What happened?" Krista pushed away the airbag then turned and stared at me with a face that was white — either from shock or airbag debris.

"We hit a — " But before I could finish my sentence, someone was opening the doors on the passenger side. A blast of cold air entered the car as a couple of men began helping the girls out and asking if anyone was seriously injured. Everyone seemed able to move and walk okay, and although I was relieved, I just couldn't hold it back anymore. Standing out on the edge of the freeway, I burst into uncontrollable tears.

Krista put her arm around me as the two men led the girls to the truck up ahead of them. "It's going to be okay, Jenna," she said soothingly. "God protected us. We could've been killed, but God protected us. Can't you see that?"

I just kept sobbing.

"Are you girls able to climb up there?" asked the burly man with the cowboy hat. "It's warm inside, and you'll be safe until help arrives."

One by one he helped all of us climb into his cab. "Emergency crews are on the way," he told us. "You stay put until they get here. There's a five-car wreck on up ahead and traffic will probably be blocked for at least an hour." Then he closed the door.

"Looks like no concert tonight," said Lucy as she pulled her cell phone out of her coat pocket and started to dial a number.

Now Anna was crying too. "I thought we were going to die," she sobbed. "I thought we were all goners."

"God was watching out for us tonight," said Krista in a surprisingly calm voice. "He protected us."

"My shoulder hurts," said Anna. "I think I might've broken something."

"I'm so sorry," I said as I wiped my nose on the sleeve of my coat. "It's all my fault."

"It's not your fault," said Lucy. "How were you supposed to know there was a wreck up ahead?"

"Or that the road was icy," said Krista.

"This could've happened to anyone," said Lucy.

But I started crying again. I knew it was my fault. Completely my fault. All four of us could've been killed tonight. And that would've been all my fault too. I was a miserable excuse for a friend and a miserable excuse of a Christian.

Now Lucy was talking on the phone to her parents, telling them what had happened but assuring them that they were okay. "Well, except for Anna. She may have hurt her shoulder. But the paramedics should be here soon."

Then Anna borrowed Lucy's phone to call her parents. And that's when I realized I still needed to tell my parents too. Unfortunately or fortunately, depending on how I looked at it, my cell phone was still in the car. The smashed-up and most likely totaled car.

Oh, how had I gotten myself into this mess? Despite the sharp pain in my neck, I leaned forward, and putting my throbbing head in my hands, I continued to sob. Why had I been so pathetically stupid?

Krista gently rubbed my back and assured me that it was going to be okay. "God is in control," said Krista. "He's watching over us, Jenna."

*Well, God might be watching over Krista, I thought, and maybe Anna and Lucy too (since Krista had been praying for both of them), but no way was God watching out for me right now. I mean, if God had been watching out for me, we never would've ended up in this wreck tonight.*

*But then I had to ask myself, why should God watch out for me? Why should he give me the time of day when I had almost completely turned my back on him? Maybe it would've been better if I'd been seriously injured. Then at least my parents might feel a tiny bit sorry for me. As it was, I knew I was in big trouble. Big stinking trouble!*

6. How good of a Christian friend is Krista right now? What about Jenna?

7. Describe a time when you helped a friend and felt really good about it.

Love from the center of who you are; don't fake it. . . .
Be good friends who love deeply; practice playing second fiddle.

Romans 12:9-10

## The Designer's Direction

Laugh with your happy friends when they're happy; share tears when
they're down. Get along with each other; don't be stuck-up.
Make friends with nobodies; don't be the great somebody.

Romans 12:15-16

## Getting Honest

8. How easy is it for you to "Make friends with nobodies" (Romans
12:16)? Why is that?

9. Do you have some good Christian friends in your life? If so,
describe what you appreciate about them. If not, what can you do
about that?

10. How good of a Christian friend are you to others? What are your strengths and weaknesses in this department?

11. What specific things can you do to make sure you're being a good friend to someone?

God wants you to take loving each other seriously. Do you know why? It's because others are watching. People who don't know God, but know you, are observing you and your Christian friends. They're trying to see if there's anything better about your life. Admit it, it's easy for people to make fun of Christians. Sometimes (like when you're being a jerk) you offer your observers a lot of good material.

But what happens when a nonbeliever sees Christians who really love and care and forgive each other in the way that God intended? That's when lives can be changed, hearts can be turned around, and God can really be glorified. Try it and see.

> Overlook an offense and bond a friendship;
> fasten on to a slight and—good-bye, friend!
> A quiet rebuke to a person of good sense
> does more than a whack on the head of a fool.
>
> Proverbs 17:9-10

Another fringe benefit of a having a good Christian friend is that it's like having a counselor in your back pocket. Oh, sure your friend might not have a degree in psychology, but if she knows you and loves you, and she knows and loves God too, she can probably give you some pretty decent advice.

Like if you're making a big decision and it doesn't seem totally clear. Why not ask some of your Christian friends (including some in leadership roles) what they think, or invite them to pray for you, or find out what they would do in a similar situation? Not that you'll make your decision solely on this advice, but when you put it alongside God's Word and what you believe he's saying to your heart — well, you can hardly go wrong with that.

## jenna's story continues . . .

*I couldn't stand it anymore. Here Krista was being so sweet and encouraging about the whole thing. She was trying to make me feel better, but she was clueless as to what was going on inside me. Krista had no idea that I had lied. Suddenly I knew I had to get this crud off my chest.*

*I turned to Krista. "It's not going to be okay. Okay?"*

*Krista blinked. "What do you mean?"*

*"I mean I borrowed my mom's car without permission. When I asked my parents earlier this week, they both said no. But they had to go to my grandma's and I was supposed to be staying with Aunt Cindy and, well, I just took the keys to the car and—" But that's as far as I got. I was crying again.*

*"No way!" said Lucy. "You borrowed your mom's car without permission?"*

*I turned to Lucy and nodded.*

*Lucy just shook her head. "Really stupid, Jenna."*

"*Seriously stupid*," said Anna. "*My parents would ground me for life if I did anything that lame.*"

*I looked down at my lap.* "*Yeah. I know.*"

"*Oh, Jenna,*" said Krista. "*I can't believe you did that. It's not even like you.*"

"*I know,*" I muttered without looking up.

"*I wish you would've told me sooner,*" said Krista. "*We could've gotten a ride with someone else, you know.*"

*I thought Krista sounded slightly angry now. Not that I could blame her — or any of them for that matter. They probably all hated me by now. The four of us just sat there in silence.*

"*Are you mad at me?*" *I finally asked in a quiet voice. Mostly I was asking Krista. But she didn't answer.*

"*I'm mad,*" said Lucy. "*I think it totally sucks that you took your mom's car without permission and then wrecked it with us in it. I hope you don't get us all into serious trouble. Like maybe the police will think we stole the vehicle or something.*"

"*I hope your parents have good insurance,*" said Anna as she rubbed her sore shoulder.

*I just sighed and wished I'd been knocked unconscious in the wreck. Like why couldn't I just wake up in some hospital room with my worried parents looking on with love and concern?*

"*What you did was wrong, Jenna,*" Krista spoke in a serious voice. "*And I can't lie to you. I'm pretty shocked and disappointed.*"

"*I know . . .* " *I kept looking at my lap.*

"*But I still love you.*" Krista put her hand on my arm. "*And so does God. And we'll both stick with you through this whole mess.*"

*But this only put a humungous lump in my throat, so big that I couldn't even speak. And now I could tell that a few more gallons of fresh tears were on their way down.*

## My Design Plan

Once again you need to realize that this is your life and this is your plan, your design. No one can do this for you. Maybe you're starting to see why God wants you to have some good Christian friends in your life. Or maybe you're still not sure.

12. Why do you need fellowship?

13. What regular forms of fellowship, if any, do you have?

14. Ask God to show you some specific ways to have more fellowship. How do you believe he's leading you?

15. What can you do right now to make sure you're getting real fellowship?

Now that you've cleaned up your lives by following the truth,
love one another as if your lives depended on it.

1 Peter 1:22

## *Journal Your Thoughts*

Choose one of the Bible passages in this chapter and write about why it's especially relevant to you. What is God saying to you? How do you feel about that? What will you do in response to this passage?

## My Design Goals

So maybe you know beyond a shadow of doubt that you need fellowship with other Christians. You know that you can't do this thing alone. You want to design your life to contain quality forms of fellowship. Not just for a week or two, but for always. What will you do to make sure this happens?

## My Fellowship Goals Are:

My dear children, let's not just talk about love;

let's practice real love.

This is the only way we'll know we're living truly,

living in God's reality.

It's also the way to shut down debilitating self-criticism,

even when there is something to it.

For God is greater than our worried hearts

and knows more about us than we do ourselves.

1 John 3:18-20

## additional bible verses on fellowship:

Ecclesiastes 4:9-12

Romans 15:7

Proverbs 3:3-4

Proverbs 27:10

Proverbs 27:17

Romans 12:13

# design discipline

So be very careful to act exactly as God commands you.
Don't veer off to the right or the left.
Walk straight down the road God commands
so that you'll have a good life and live a long time
in the land that you're about to possess.

Deuteronomy 5:32-33

*M*ost people don't like the sound of the word *discipline*. That is, unless you're training for a marathon or studying for SATs or trying to lose a few pounds. Then you probably have a basic understanding that some forms of discipline can actually be beneficial. But without discipline of any kind, you get lazy and sloppy and prone to failure — in other words, you turn into a loser.

But whether you realize it or not, you've probably already established some daily disciplines. Maybe you take them for granted because they've turned into just ordinary habits. For instance, you've probably developed the discipline to get out of bed in the morning — okay, at least on school days. And you probably brush your teeth and make it to school on time. Those are all forms of discipline. And without those disciplined habits, you'd be in serious trouble, right? As in your parents would be furious, your grades would stink, and your teeth would be rotting out of your head.

So maybe you can look at discipline as a positive thing — something that can transport you from a ho-hum, whatever kind of life to the next level, a life that's worth looking forward to.

Discipline is essential for following God. Because, as you probably know by now, *serving God doesn't "just happen."* It's not something you just roll out of bed and naturally do. In fact, you face an onslaught of distractions and roadblocks that attempt to discourage you from following God.

So when the going gets tough (and it will), you can be glad that you've invited discipline into your life. Just like that marathon runner as she crosses the finish line, you will appreciate the value of all your hard work, training, and daily disciplines.

GOD proves to be good to the man who passionately waits,
to the woman who diligently seeks.
It's a good thing to quietly hope,
quietly hope for help from GOD.
It's a good thing when you're young
to stick it out through the hard times.
When life is heavy and hard to take,
go off by yourself. Enter the silence.
Bow in prayer. Don't ask questions:
Wait for hope to appear.

Lamentations 3:25-29

1. Take a look at Lamentations 3:25-29. The guy who wrote this poem had just lost his city to invasion, slaughter, rape, starvation — really bad stuff. If you read the rest of the poem in the Bible, you'll see that this guy had no trouble telling God exactly how he felt about the situation. What do you think about the way he handled his grief?

2. How do you deal with bad stuff in your life?

3. How would you like to deal with it?

Perhaps you've been making some disciplined choices and you're beginning to see the payoff. Maybe you're feeling better about yourself, God, and others around you. Maybe you're feeling more hopeful about your future in general. And maybe you're starting to realize that you actually *do* have a design for your life — and you're excited about what comes next.

That's fantastic. But one of the keys to following God — and doing it successfully and consistently — is remembering *it's a daily thing.* Not so unlike getting out of bed, brushing your teeth, and making it to class on time. You just gotta do it. And you gotta do it again and again and again.

Love GOD, your God, with your whole heart:
love him with all that's in you, love him with all you've got!

Write these commandments that I've given you today on your hearts.
Get them inside of you. . . . Talk about them wherever you are,
sitting at home or walking in the street;
talk about them from the time you get up in the morning
to when you fall into bed at night.
Tie them on your hands and foreheads as a reminder;
inscribe them on the doorposts of your homes and on your city gates.
Deuteronomy 6:5-9

4. In Deuteronomy 6:5-9, God makes a big deal about talking about his commands — even suggesting you write them on your hands. Why do you think it's so important?

5.  How can you make God's commands part of your everyday life?

Does it really take discipline to love God? Like don't you just love him because you love him? Well, of course. But, like any relationship, days will come when you don't really *feel* very loving. Maybe you don't feel very anything — like *why doesn't everyone just leave me alone today?* And that's where *you have to step from the "feeling" side of loving over to the "committed" side of loving.* That's when you have to remind yourself that even if you're having a bad day or feeling bummed about something, you're still committed to loving God — with your whole heart. And that takes discipline.

> You've all been to the stadium and seen the athletes race.
> Everyone runs; one wins. Run to win. All good athletes train hard.
> They do it for a gold medal that tarnishes and fades.
> You're after one that's gold eternally.
>
> I don't know about you, but I'm running hard for the finish line.
> I'm giving it everything I've got. No sloppy living for me!
> I'm staying alert and in top condition. I'm not going to get caught napping,
> telling everyone else all about it and then missing out myself.
>
> 1 Corinthians 9:24-27

6. What's one area of your life where you're disciplined? Maybe you work hard at a sport. Maybe you have a favorite show that you never miss. Maybe you never show up at school without great hair! There has to be something. Write down one area and what motivates you to work so hard at it.

## Design in Progress

Some people try to appear disciplined. They might go to church or youth group or attend a weekly Bible study or participate in volunteer projects, but everything they do is only on the surface. They are performing for others to see. Don't fall into that trap. God wants you to serve him with an honest heart. He wants your discipline to emerge from the relationship you're sharing with him — daily. He doesn't want you to be a fake. He wants you to be real — in the same way that he is real.

Don't fool yourself into thinking that you are a listener when
you are anything but, letting the Word go in one ear and out the other.
*Act* on what you hear!
Those who hear and don't act are like those who glance in the mirror,
walk away, and two minutes later have no idea
who they are, what they look like.
James 1:22-24

## jenna's story continues . . .

*Paramedics arrived and transported all four of us to the hospital. I wasn't sure it was really necessary in my case, but I wasn't about to argue. Besides, I was eager to get away from the wreck site. It was just too depressing.*

*After being examined by the ER doctor, I was given some pills for pain and released. "Make sure you make an appointment with your regular doctor next week," the doctor advised me. "You probably have a minor case of whiplash."*

*Anna had a broken collarbone, and both Lucy and Krista were basically fine. Just bruised and sore.*

*"You girls were lucky," the doctor told me. "It could've been much worse."*

*"Yeah, right." I sighed as I picked up my coat. I knew it was time to call my parents. But what was I going to tell them? After standing and staring at the pay phone for about five minutes, I finally decided to call Aunt Cindy. Without saying exactly whose car had been in the wreck, I relayed the bad news to my aunt.*

*"I haven't called Mom and Dad yet," I admitted. "My cell phone's still in the car and I'm at the hospital now. This is the first chance I've had to call anyone."*

*"Do you want me to call them?" offered my aunt.*

*"Would you?" I said eagerly. "That'd be great."*

*"And how about if we come pick you up," said Aunt Cindy. "I don't think you should be spending the night at Krista's in light of all this."*

*I agreed and hung up. Then leaning my head against the phone, I did something that I hadn't done for what seemed like days, but was actually only hours. I prayed.*

*"I'm sorry, God," I whispered in this semiprivate space. "I know I*

wasn't listening to you these past couple of days. I know that I disobeyed you, as well as my parents. I know that it's totally my fault my mom's car got wrecked tonight. And I'm sorry, God. I'm really, really sorry." I was crying again, but no longer with the hopeless hysteria I'd felt earlier. Then I actually thanked God that the wreck hadn't been worse and I asked him to forgive me and to help me with my parents. Not that I wanted to escape whatever punishment was coming my way. I just didn't want them to be too upset or worried.

"How's it going?" asked Krista as she emerged from ER.

"Okay." I blew my nose on a tissue and forced a little smile. "Thanks for everything tonight, Krista. You're a really good friend."

Then we hugged and Krista assured me that everything was going to be okay. "Lucy's parents are already here," she said, then pointing down the hallway. "And here come Anna's now."

"How's Anna feeling?" I asked.

"Fine, now that they gave her some pain meds. She said she's going to have to wear some kind of a neck brace thingie."

I just shook my head. "I think I should go say something to her parents." So I approached Anna's parents and quickly told them that I was very sorry and that I'd been the driver. Then I asked if they needed any insurance information.

"Don't worry about that now," said Anna's dad. "We've already talked to Anna on the phone, and we're just glad no one got seriously hurt."

"Where's Anna now?" asked her mom with a worried expression. So Krista and I took them to see their daughter. It wasn't long before the other parents and Aunt Cindy were all gathered in the waiting area, getting ready to leave. And that's when I decided to just make a clean break and confess everything. I knew I would look stupid and irresponsible, but I *just sensed that God was telling me to do this.*

*"I need to tell you all something," I began in a serious voice. "I was the driver tonight, but I didn't have permission to drive my mom's car. I'm really sorry that we got in the wreck, and it probably never would've happened if I'd been doing what I should've been doing." I sighed. "Like staying home."*

*Although the parents (especially Aunt Cindy) seemed pretty surprised, they were also fairly understanding. And soon everyone was heading for home.*

*"I had no idea you were the driver," said Aunt Cindy as we walked to the parking lot. "Your parents are in for quite a little shock."*

*"Yeah."*

*Then I prayed silently as Aunt Cindy drove. I asked God to lead me through whatever was ahead and then I thanked him again for watching over us tonight. And to my surprise, I felt that old sense of peace returning to me. Like no matter how bad it went with my parents, at least I had God to hold onto. And that was worth a lot!*

You blow it sometimes. You can't help it. You're human, right? But God loves you enough not to let you get away with crud. Oh, you might think you can—at least for a while. But it catches up with you eventually.

God promises that *life will go better for you if you choose to obey him.* And it's much easier to obey him when you discipline yourself to spend time with him and learn his Word and enjoy hanging with your Christian brothers and sisters. He doesn't promise that life will be perfect and nothing will ever go wrong, but he does promise that he'll be there — that he'll get you through it and you'll be stronger and wiser when it's all said and done.

7. How would Jenna's life have gone better if she had a disciplined habit of listening to God?

8. If you have a disciplined life but still get into a bad car accident that isn't even your fault, do you think God has broken his end of a bargain? What makes you say that?

> Don't miss a word of this—I'm telling you how to live well,
> I'm telling you how to live at your best. . . .
>
> You'll only hear true and right words from my mouth;
> not one syllable will be twisted or skewed.
>
> You'll recognize this as true—you with open minds;
> truth-ready minds will see it at once.
>
> Proverbs 8:6,8-9

## Getting Honest

9. Do you believe that God really has your best interests at heart? Why or why not?

10. What does the word *discipline* mean to you?

11. How do you feel about the word *discipline*?

12. Do you want to become more disciplined? Why or why not?

13. Do you see any specific areas in your life where you lack discipline? If so, what are they?

14. Write a prayer to God either asking him to help you become more disciplined in specific areas, or telling him why you're not interested in discipline at this time.

Practically everything that goes on in the world—
wanting your own way, wanting everything for yourself,
wanting to appear important—has nothing to do with the Father. It
just isolates you from him.
The world and all its wanting, wanting, wanting is on the way out—
but whoever does what God wants is set for eternity.

1 John 2:16-17

## My Design Plan

God's ways are different from the world's ways. Where the world goes for the quick fix and easy answers, God's way usually requires work and commitment. And the world offers you "rewards" that look tempting at first but soon deteriorate into garbage. God's rewards turn out to be even better than they first appeared, and better yet, they last forever.

But it takes time and discipline to figure these things out. Time spent with God and the discipline of getting into his Word—over and over—again and again.

So does that sound redundant or boring to you? Think about it: Do you ever enjoy a good meal? Well, how many times a day do you eat? Does eating seem redundant or boring to you? Unless you're anorexic or ill, it probably doesn't. You know your body needs the nourishment, and besides, a cheese pizza can taste pretty good.

Well, why should it be any different with God? Your spirit needs God's nourishment, and time spent with him usually leaves you feeling pretty good. In other words, it's not boring.

15. Do you struggle with any of these: "wanting your own way, wanting everything for yourself, wanting to appear important" (1 John 2:16)? What's that like for you?

So you're almost to the end of this book now. Do you feel like you're starting to establish a life by design? Do you have hope for your future? Do you see how you're actually starting to have some control over your life?

Whatever happens to your design plan from here on out is *completely up to you*. Whether you close this book and forget about everything you've read or you make it a vital part of your life is completely up to you. Your design is in your hands.

## jenna's story ends . . .

*Of course, my parents were not too pleased to find out that not only had their "trustworthy" daughter been in a serious wreck but she'd also disobeyed them and totaled one of their cars in the process. I confessed the whole story to them, in detail, when they got back home the next day. It had been Aunt Cindy's idea to wait. "No need to worry them into thinking they need to rush home during this horrible weather," she'd told me at the hospital. "It won't change anything to wait."*

*"I can't believe you would do something like that to us," said my mother for like the hundredth time. "That is so unlike you, Jenna."*

*And for about the hundredth time, I said, "Yeah, I know, Mom. And I'm really, really sorry. I'll do whatever you want to make up for it. You can ground me until I graduate. I can be on KP duty for the rest of my life. Mow the lawn until I'm twenty-one. Whatever."*

*"I'm just relieved that no one was seriously injured," said my dad.*

*"I've been thinking about replacing that car," admitted my mom. "Not that it gets you off the hook, young lady!"*

*"I know," I said. But I did feel a small ripple of relief.*

*"Did you learn anything through all of this?" asked my dad.*

*I swallowed and nodded. "Yeah."*

*"And that is?" My mother looked expectantly at me.*

*"To listen to God," I said. "To obey him in everything."*

*My dad nodded and my mom seemed satisfied.*

*"So am I grounded or what?" I asked, eager to get the punishment portion of my stupidity out of the way.*

*"We'll let you know," said my dad in a serious tone.*

*"That's right," agreed my mom. "We need to discuss it."*

*"Whatever . . . " I said. "In the meantime, I'll go clean the kitchen." But as I cleaned the kitchen (a chore I normally dislike), I felt a powerful sense of relief. And even though I knew my parents would come up with some kind of punishment, I really wasn't that worried because I was certain that it couldn't be half as bad as the way I felt when I turned my back on God. And hopefully I wouldn't have to learn my next life lesson the hard way.*

Put into practice what you learned from me, what you heard and saw and realized. Do that, and God, who makes everything work together, will work you into his most excellent harmonies.

Philippians 4:9

## Journal Your Thoughts

How do you feel about Philippians 4:9? Do you think it's true? Do you want it to be part of your life? Journal about how this verse makes you feel inside.

## My Final Goals

Okay, it's time to look back over what you've been learning about devotion, prayer, fellowship, and discipline. What goals can you create that cover all four of these foundational truths? For instance you might want to pick a specific time of day for a daily appointment with God. Or maybe you want to start keeping a prayer list or partnering with some friends to pray. Maybe you need to commit yourself to join a fellowship group, or maybe to invite someone to come with you to the group you already attend. Whatever your goals are, write them in a way that makes them practical and doable:

1.

2.

3.

4.

You might also want to write these goals on a card that you can tape to your mirror or keep in your pocket. And when you're done, don't forget to take a moment to commit these goals to God. Ask him to guide you and to help you realize these goals.

So let's do it—full of belief, confident that we're presentable
inside and out. Let's keep a firm grip on the promises that
keep us going. He always keeps his word.

Hebrews 10:22-23

## additional bible verses on discipline:

1 Peter 2:16

Romans 8:37-39

# one

## Check out this chapter from
## *Dark Blue*—Book 1 of Melody Carlson's
## TrueColors series.

Jordan Ferguson *used* to be my best friend. Now she makes me sick. Just hearing her name called out in first period English or seeing her flitting down the hall with her lame new friends makes me want to hurl. Really!

And comments like, "Oh, Jordan, I totally love your hair today," or, "Hey, Jordan, that outfit is really hot," actually make me want to hit something. I mean *puh-leeze*, these are the exact same girls Jordan and I *used* to make fun of. Behind their backs anyway—it's not like we were ignorant. At least I'm not. I can't speak for Jordan—not anymore.

Not that I ever did speak for Jordan. No, she's always been perfectly capable of doing that herself. The sorry truth is, whether I liked it or not, she often spoke for me too. I guess it all started way back in kindergarten. My parents had recently divorced and I thought their problems were all my fault. As a result I think I was feeling pretty insecure and probably scared too. I didn't want to talk to anyone and made a point of hanging out on the sidelines and keeping my little mouth shut. But one day our kindergarten teacher Miss March asked, "Who wants to play with the puppet theater next?" And even though I was dying to put my hand inside of that plump pink Miss Piggy puppet, I couldn't utter a single word. I nearly fell over when this tiny blonde girl wearing a mint-green My Little Pony sweatshirt walked over and took me by the hand.

"Kara Hendricks and I want to do the puppets now," she said in this great big voice that totally contradicted her size. Jordan was the smallest girl in the class back then. Even now she's barely five feet tall in her socks. But how she actually knew, at the age of five, not only my first but also my last name was a complete mystery to me. So naturally I didn't argue with her. I even managed to find my voice once I was safely behind the puppet theater curtain and my hand was tucked into the bright-green Kermit the Frog puppet. Naturally, Jordan wanted Miss Piggy for herself. And who was I to question the girl who helped me step outside of myself for a change? Not having Miss Piggy seemed a pretty small sacrifice. After that, Jordan did most of the talking for both of us, especially during that first year. Oh, I would talk to her, but only in this quiet mousy voice. Then she would speak to the teacher or a classmate or whoever until my wants and needs were perfectly clear. It's like I was the hand puppet and she was the puppeteer. Still, her outgoing personality made life much easier for me.

Fortunately, I did get better at speaking, over time. But I've never been what you might call an assertive or even confident person. And I would never in a million years want to speak in public on purpose. Jordan, on the other hand, loved her speech class last year and even joined the debate team, and she was only a freshman! But I don't get it. I mean why would anyone willingly put themselves into a position where they have to speak in front of an audience *and* argue about something? How whacked out is that?

Still, I admit that I admired her for it. I thought she was the bravest and coolest person I knew. And throughout our freshman year in high school, just last year, I was totally thankful that I had Jordan Ferguson to share a locker, walk down the halls, eat lunch, and just basically hang with. She was like my security blanket. Well, that and a lot more.

I suppose that's why losing her like this is so freaking crappy. Not that I'll ever admit *that*. Not to her or anyone else in this moronic school. As it is, my life already sucks. I don't need anyone's stupid pity to add to my stinking pile of misery. Besides, I do a pretty good job of feeling sorry for myself.

"What's up with you and Jordan?" my teenybopper sister asked the other day. "How come she never comes 'round here anymore?"

Naturally, Bree *would* miss Jordan. She thinks Jordan's the coolest thing next to (gag me) Britney Spears. Just the same, I rolled my eyes at her and said, "Probably because you're such a total stink bomb. Poor Jordan just couldn't take your smell anymore."

Of course, this led to a rip-snorting argument about hygiene and fashion and a bunch of other things Bree and I don't quite agree on. Turned out to be a good distraction—Bree hasn't mentioned Jordan's absence since. Still, I'm sure she privately wonders. You'd think my mom might wonder too, but as usual she's so into her own world that she is totally clueless about mine. So what's new?

But I guess I sort of wish my mom would ask me about it. Now tell me that's not weird, since I usually don't want to talk (I mean *talk)* to my mom about anything besides lunch money or whose turn it is to clean the kitchen. I guess that just shows how completely desperate I am.

I sort of feel like I'm drowning here, and I just keep wishing that someone—anyone—would toss me a life preserver, or even a rope . . . maybe to hang myself with. Because I really need someone to talk to. The pathetic thing is, the only person I've ever poured my heart out to before, the only one who's ever listened or attempted to give me answers, the only one who knew how to make me feel better, just doesn't give a rip.

As furious as I am with Jordan, and as much as I can't stand the very sight of her, I still miss her friendship more than I imagined possible, and I think I'd do almost anything to get her back. As lame as it sounds, even to me, there's a great big gaping hole in my life right now. And I feel more alone than ever.

Not to mention scared.

# author

Melody Carlson has written dozens of books for all age groups, but she particularly enjoys writing for teens. Perhaps this is because her own teen years remain so vivid in her memory. After claiming to be an atheist at the ripe old age of twelve, she later surrendered her heart to Jesus and has been following him ever since. Her hope and prayer for all her readers is that each one would be touched by God in a special way through her stories. For more information, visit Melody's website at www.melodycarlson.com.

# DISCOVER A UNIQUE NEW KIND OF BIBLE STUDY.

How did Jesus teach many of his most important lessons? He told stories. That's the idea behind the first series of Bible studies from best-selling fiction author Melody Carlson. In each of the four studies, Melody weaves fictional stories with practical discussion questions to get you thinking about some of the most important topics in life: your relationship with God, your relationship with others, identity, and forgiveness.

## Finding Out Who You Really Are
1576837262

## Making the Most of Your Relationships
1576837270

## Discovering a Forgiveness Plan
1576837289

Visit your local Christian bookstore,
call NavPress at 1-800-366-7788, or log on to www.navpress.com
to purchase.

To locate a Christian bookstore near you,
call 1-800-991-7747.

NAVPRESS
BRINGING TRUTH TO LIFE
www.navpress.com

THINK

TH1NK Books
an imprint of NavPress®